# CODING BASICS

by George Anthony Kulz

FOCUS READERS

# WWW.FOCUSREADERS.COM

Focus Readers is distributed by North Star Editions:
sales@northstareditions.com | 888-417-0195

Produced for Focus Readers by Red Line Editorial.

Content Consultant: Dr. Sherali Zeadally, Associate Professor, College of Communication and Information, University of Kentucky

Photographs ©: Aksonsat Uanthoeng/Shutterstock Images, cover, 1; Wayhome Studio/Shutterstock Images, 4–5; metamorworks/Shutterstock Images, 7; Redpixel.pl/Shutterstock Images, 8–9; PureSolution/Shutterstock Images, 10; California Institute of Technology/JPL/NASA, 12–13; Balakate/Shutterstock Images, 14–15; Monstar Studio/Shutterstock Images, 17; Red Line Editorial, 19; AngieYeoh/Shutterstock Images, 20–21; Zapp2Photo/Shutterstock Images, 22; Dragon Images/Shutterstock Images, 24–25; Gorodenkoff/Shutterstock Images, 27; Kanut Srinin/Shutterstock Images, 29

**Library of Congress Cataloging-in-Publication Data**
Library of Congress Cataloging-in-Publication Data is available on the Library of Congress website.

**ISBN**
978-1-64185-326-2 (hardcover)
978-1-64185-384-2 (paperback)
978-1-64185-500-6 (ebook pdf)
978-1-64185-442-9 (hosted ebook)

Printed in the United States of America
Mankato, MN
October, 2018

## ABOUT THE AUTHOR

George Anthony Kulz holds a master's degree in computer engineering. He is a member of the Society of Children's Book Writers and Illustrators and has taken courses at the Institute of Children's Literature and the Gotham Writers' Workshop. He writes for children and adults.

# TABLE OF CONTENTS

**CHAPTER 1**

All Kinds of Computers  5

**CHAPTER 2**

What Code Can Do  9

## CODING IN ACTION

Tracking Data  12

**CHAPTER 3**

The Coding Process  15

**CHAPTER 4**

Code at Work  21

**CHAPTER 5**

Coding Careers  25

Focus on Coding Basics • 30
Glossary • 31
To Learn More • 32
Index • 32

# ALL KINDS OF COMPUTERS

An alarm beeps. Two sisters wake up. One taps her phone's screen to turn off the alarm. The other uses her phone to check the weather. Then both girls get ready for school. In the kitchen, their dad cooks breakfast and drinks coffee. The coffee was ready before he got up. The coffeemaker made it while he was asleep.

A smartphone is actually a tiny computer.

After breakfast, the girls walk to the bus stop. Their dad leaves for work. The house locks all the doors and windows. It uses sensors to watch for movement. If someone tries to break in, the system will alert the police.

All these devices depend on code. Code is a set of instructions that tell a computer what to do. Each device has a computer inside. The computer controls the device. But the computer must be given instructions. Code tells the computer how to complete each step of its task. For example, code tells the coffeemaker's computer what time to start making the coffee.

Code helps a self-driving car reach its destination.

Devices that use code can be found in many places. People use them at work, at school, and in their homes. **Appliances** often use code. So do devices that people can wear, such as smartwatches. The devices help people do their jobs and find information. Code can even help control vehicles.

SIDEBAR
SOCIAL MEDIA

ME

...lace for your text. Post here everything that is related to your business.
...u care, what are the best. Your achievements. Give details of operations.
...e greatest achievement.

...npanies cooperating with us located here.
...d of the description invite you to read the rest of the tabs.

WEBSITE

LOGO

HOME | NEWS | GALLERY | CONTACT

IMAGE

SIDEBAR

TEXT

# CHAPTER 2

# WHAT CODE CAN DO

**P**eople often use code to create programs. A program is a set of instructions that are given to a machine so it can perform an action. There are many kinds of programs. Each one does a specific task. For example, a word processor is a program that people can use to write and edit text.

All computer programs and websites are made possible by code.

Programs are often designed to solve problems. Code breaks each problem down into step-by-step instructions. Many programs are created for laptops, tablets, and smartphones. But computers are part of other devices, too. Robots,

## COMMON PROGRAMS

**Antivirus:** protects against harmful code

**Design:** creates and edits images

**Web browser:** displays websites

**Database:** stores and searches data

**Messaging:** sends and receives messages

**Operating system:** runs a computer or device

**drones**, and cars all have computers inside them. They use programs as well.

The internet also uses code. When a person visits a website, code makes the images and text appear. Code also allows people to share information online. It controls how devices send and receive information.

## MAKING A WEB PAGE

Many websites use a kind of code called HyperText Markup Language (HTML). This code is not used to create programs. Instead, it controls how a web page will look. Coders use HTML to change the text's size and color. They can also create **links**. Clicking on a link takes a user to a different web page.

# TRACKING DATA

Data is information collected to study or track something. Some computers store huge amounts of data. However, large amounts of information are hard for people to work with. People might struggle to find the data they want. Or they might not understand how information is related.

Computers use code to organize data. They can find information much faster than people can. Computers can also recognize patterns. For example, the Large Synoptic Survey Telescope will take pictures of outer space. Each picture will contain a huge amount of data. Code will send alerts to scientists when important objects in the pictures change. By studying the changes, scientists will learn more about the universe.

The Large Synoptic Survey Telescope will help scientists track billions of stars.

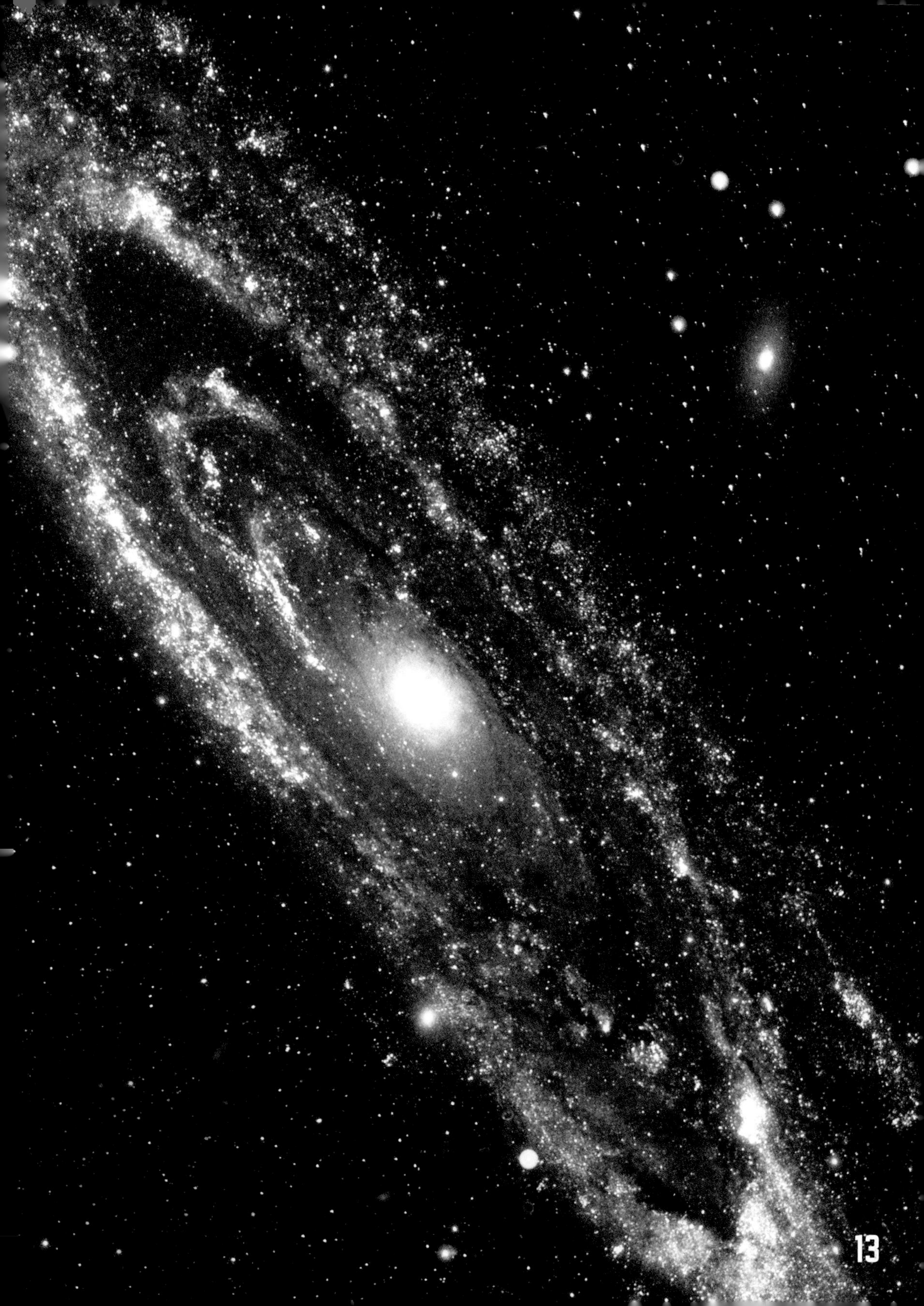

# CHAPTER 3

# THE CODING PROCESS

**P**eople who write code are called programmers. Writing code involves several steps. First, programmers identify a problem to solve. For instance, suppose students want to guide a robot through a maze. They could write a program that tells the robot how to move.

Code gives a robot step-by-step instructions to complete a task.

Next, programmers break the problem down into goals. They divide each goal into several steps. For example, the students would want their robot to avoid hitting walls. This goal could have three steps. First, the robot would stop when it neared a wall. Next, the robot would turn. Third, it would move in another direction.

Programmers write out all the steps to solve the problem. This list of steps is known as an algorithm. Programmers translate each step of the algorithm into code. They write instructions in a programming language.

There are hundreds of programming languages. Computers only understand

```
continue;
}
float du = (tiles[i] % 16) * s;
float dv = (tiles[i] / 16) * s;
int flip = ao[i][0] + ao[i][3] > ao[i][1] + ao[i][2];
for (int v = 0; v < 6; v++) {
    int j = flip ? flipped[i][v] : indices[i][v];
    *(d++) = x + n * positions[i][j][0];
    *(d++) = y + n * positions[i][j][1];
    *(d++) = z + n * positions[i][j][2];
    *(d++) = normals[i][0];
    *(d++) = normals[i][1];
    *(d++) = normals[i][2];
    *(d++) = du + (uvs[i][j][0] ? b : a);
    *(d++) = dv + (uvs[i][j][1] ? b : a);
    *(d++) = ao[i][j];
    *(d++) = light[i][j];
}
}
}
}

void make_cube(
    float *data, float ao[6][4], float light[6][4],
    int left, int right, int top, int bottom, int front, int back,
    float x, float y, float z, float n, int w)
{
    int wleft = blocks[w][0];
    int wright = blocks[w][1];
    int wtop = blocks[w][2];
    int wbottom = blocks[w][3];
    int wfront = blocks[w][4];
    int wback = blocks[w][5];
    make_cube_faces(
        data, ao, light,
        left, right, top, bottom, front, back,
        wleft, wright, wtop, wbottom, wfront, wback,
```

C is a popular programming language because it makes writing commands easy.

machine language, but this language is hard for humans to use. So, most programmers write their code in other programming languages. The code will be translated into machine language later.

Either a **compiler** or an **interpreter** does this step. These two kinds of programs change the instructions to a format the computer can understand.

Finally, programmers **run** and test their program. They make sure it works as they planned. If it doesn't, they try to fix it.

## COMPUTER TALK

Machine language is made up of ones and zeroes. These numbers control electric pulses that happen inside the computer. A one sends a pulse. A zero does not. Making a pattern of zeroes and ones controls how the computer sends information. But writing instructions with only zeroes and ones can take a long time. Usually, people choose programming languages that are easier to write.

They change the code or the algorithm.
Then they test the program again.

Programmers continue testing and
fixing until the code does what they
want. Then the program is ready for other
people to use.

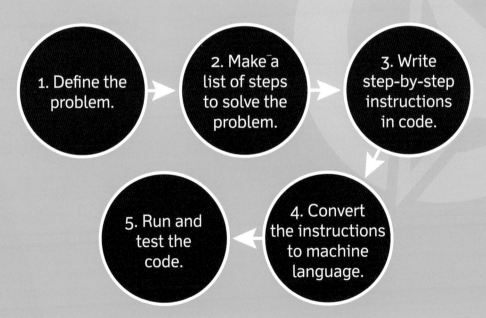

## STEPS TO WRITING CODE

1. Define the problem.

2. Make a list of steps to solve the problem.

3. Write step-by-step instructions in code.

4. Convert the instructions to machine language.

5. Run and test the code.

# CHAPTER 4

# CODE AT WORK

**A**fter people write code for a program, the code can be used many times. The code will run every time the program is used. In most cases, the code includes instructions for how to respond to the user. It often waits for the user to perform an action. For example, if a person taps a cell phone **app**, the app will open.

Code tells a map app which route to display.

A robot scans each box to help a company keep track of its products.

An action that a computer responds to is known as an event.

Some devices need instructions from users. But the users don't typically need to know code. For example, a robot vacuum cleaner needs to know when to start and stop. Users can push buttons on the vacuum. The vacuum's computer changes this information into code.

Other devices follow programs that are already written. Robots in factories are one example. These robots are programmed to do one task. They repeat the same steps over and over.

## AT THE FACTORY

The first programmable factory robot was invented in the 1950s. It lifted and stacked hot metal parts. Today, factories all over the world use robots. Robots help with many jobs, such as building car parts. The robots do these jobs faster than people can. They also do work that is too hard or dangerous for people.

# CHAPTER 5

# CODING CAREERS

Because code has so many uses, almost every company needs programmers. Some programmers make websites. Others create new programs. All of them must know how to code. Many people study coding in college. They take different classes based on what job they hope to do.

Programming is among the fastest-growing careers in the United States.

Computer science is the most common coding degree. Students learn how to write code to solve problems. They study different programming languages. They learn how to write instructions in each one. People with this degree can work for a wide variety of companies.

In software engineering, students learn to write programs and requirements. Requirements are lists of rules. The rules help programs solve a problem. For example, an ATM is a machine that lets people get money from their bank accounts. The ATM must know how much money is in each person's account. Knowing this amount is a requirement.

Software engineers create programs for smartphones.

Software engineers also learn to test and **install** code. They often get jobs making programs or websites. Some even create video games.

Other programmers study information systems. In this field, people learn how to organize and manage data for companies.

They learn about the data companies need and how the companies use it. They also learn how to protect the data. They design code that makes the data difficult for **hackers** to steal.

Computer engineers focus on the computers inside devices. They learn about code and the computers it runs on. They study how computers interact with other devices. In addition, they learn how people interact with computers.

Some computer engineers write code that helps people use computers. Others write code that helps devices interact with one another. Sometimes these devices join together to create systems.

Some devices use code to share information about a person's health.

For instance, sensors in an alarm system use code to share information.

Some people study more than just coding. Video game coders may study art and animation. People who write code for robots may learn how robots move and are built. As more devices use code, companies will need programmers more than ever. Coding careers will continue to grow quickly.

# FOCUS ON
# CODING BASICS

*Write your answers on a separate piece of paper.*

1. Write a sentence summarizing the main ideas in Chapter 4.

2. What type of coding career would you most want to have? Why would you choose that one?

3. What is the first step in the coding process?

    **A.** The programmer creates an algorithm.
    **B.** The programmer identifies a problem to solve.
    **C.** The programmer runs and tests the code.

4. What is the main goal of an algorithm?

    **A.** to solve a problem by using a set of instructions
    **B.** to teach more people how to write machine code
    **C.** to identify and fix mistakes in a program's code

*Answer key on page 32.*

# GLOSSARY

**app**
A computer program that completes a task.

**appliances**
Machines that have specific jobs, such as stoves or fans.

**compiler**
A program that turns all the code in a program into machine language at one time.

**drones**
Aircraft or ships that are controlled remotely or operate on their own.

**hackers**
People who illegally access computers.

**install**
To put code onto the device that will run a program.

**interpreter**
A program that turns code into machine language one line at a time.

**links**
Connections between two web pages or two websites.

**run**
To start a program and have it perform the task it was written to do.

# TO LEARN MORE

## BOOKS

Edelman, Brad. *Computer Programming: Learn It, Try It!* North Mankato, MN: Capstone Press, 2018.

Nagelhout, Ryan. *Smart Machines and the Internet of Things*. New York: Rosen Publishing, 2015.

Smibert, Angie. *All About Coding*. Lake Elmo, MN: Focus Readers, 2017.

## NOTE TO EDUCATORS

Visit **www.focusreaders.com** to find lesson plans, activities, links, and other resources related to this title.

# INDEX

algorithm, 16, 19
app, 21

computer, 6, 10–11, 12, 16, 18, 22–23, 28
computer engineering, 28
computer science, 26

data, 10, 12, 27–28

event, 22

hackers, 28
HTML, 11

information systems, 27–28
internet, 11

machine language, 17–19

programming language, 16–18, 26

robot, 10, 15–16, 22–23, 29

sensors, 6, 29
software engineering, 26–27

testing, 18–19, 27

website, 10–11, 25, 27
word processor, 9

**Answer Key: 1.** Answers will vary; **2.** Answers will vary; **3.** B; **4.** A